Shops

Written by Roderick Hunt
Illustrated by Alex Brychta

OXFORD

UNIVERSITY PRESS

Read these words

shop   ship

shell   shed

shut   shall

Sam had a shop.

"I sell shells," she said.

Pam had a shop.

"This is a ship shop,"
she said.

Pat had a hat shop.

"I sell hats," she said.

"Then I will get a hat,"
said Kipper.

"Shall I get that big hat ...

... this cap ...

... that red hat ...

... this top hat?"

"This shop is shut,"
said Tom.

14

"This is a pan shop,"
said Tim.

"I sell pans," he said.

"I will get that pan,"
said Kipper.

"This shed is a shop,"
said Chip.

"It is a bun shop," said Biff.

"Buns," said Kipper.

Talk about the story

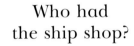
What did
Sam sell in
her shop?

Who had
the ship shop?

Which shop
would you
like to visit?

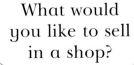
What would
you like to sell
in a shop?

21

What's in the picture?

What can you find in the picture that begins
with *sh, p, d, b, g, h?*